CANADA
After 1775, thousands of people loyal to ENGLAND came here.

LAKE ERIE

The THIRTEEN BRITISH COLONIES of North America
1775 population: 2,000,000

The native peoples were driven westward.

In 1763, PARLIAMENT told the colonists not to settle west of this line.

PENNSYLVANIA
The first colonists here were from SWEDEN

MARYLAND

BALTIMORE

VIRGINIA

WILLIAMSBURG

JAMESTOWN was the first ENGLISH settlement.
1607

NORTH CAROLINA

SOUTH CAROLINA

SWISS and GERMAN settlers founded NEWBERN 1710

CAPE FEAR

ROANOKE ISLAND
ENGLAND'S Lost Colony 1585

GEORGIA

founded in 1670 and named after King Charles II

CHARLES TOWN

The CREEK INDIANS helped the ENGLISH settlers in 1732.

SAVANNAH

The SPANISH founded St. Augustine 1565

N

QUEBEC

Until 1763, this land was under FRENCH control.

LAKE ONTARIO

IROQUOIS TERRITORY

This land was claimed by both N.Y. and N.H.

This land was part of MASSACHUSETTS BAY COLONY. On march 15th, 1820, the state of MAINE joined the UNION.

NEW HAMPSHIRE

NEW YORK

DUTCH settlers came here in 1624

PORTSMOUTH

MASSACHUSETTS

BOSTON

The PILGRIMS landed here in 1620.

CONNECTICUT

PLYMOUTH

NEW HAVEN

NEW YORK CITY

LONG ISLAND

PHILADELPHIA

ATLANTIC OCEAN

TRENTON

NEW JERSEY

DELAWARE

SWEDISH colonists built the first cabins made of logs here in 1638

Young John Quincy

by CHERYL HARNESS

—◦◦◦—

BRADBURY PRESS   New York

Maxwell Macmillan Canada   Toronto
Maxwell Macmillan International
New York   Oxford   Singapore   Sydney

I wish to acknowledge the lives and letters of John and Abigail,
the assistance of Barbara Lalicki, who edited this book,
and the staff of the Adams National Historic Site,
Quincy, Massachusetts, for their help in researching this project.
—Cheryl Harness

Bradbury Press
Macmillan Publishing Company
866 Third Avenue
New York, NY 10022

Maxwell Macmillan Canada, Inc.
1200 Eglinton Avenue East
Suite 200
Don Mills, Ontario M3C 3N1

Macmillan Publishing Company is part of the Maxwell
Communication Group of Companies.

First edition
Printed and bound in the U.S.A. on recycled paper

10 9 8 7 6 5 4 3 2 1
The text of this book is set in Janson.
Typography by Julie Quan

LIBRARY OF CONGRESS CATALOGING-IN-PUBLICATION DATA

Harness, Cheryl.
Young John Quincy / by Cheryl Harness.—1st ed.
p.   cm.
Includes bibliographical references.
Summary: Presents the events leading up to the Declaration of
Independence as seen through the eyes of the boy who would grow up
to be the sixth president of the United States.
ISBN 0-02-742644-0
1. Adams, John Quincy, 1767–1848—Juvenile literature.
2. Presidents—United States—Biography—Juvenile literature.
3. United States. Declaration of Independence—Juvenile literature.
4. United States—Politics and government—Revolution, 1775–1783—
Juvenile literature. [1. Adams, John Quincy, 1767–1848—Childhood
and youth. 2. Presidents. 3. United States—History—Revolution,
1775–1783.]
E377.H36 1994
973.5'5'092—dc20   [B]   92-37266

*This book is dedicated to my nephew, Joshua, in
honor of the Founders.
They didn't know how it was going to turn out.
We have that in common with them.*

★ PROLOGUE ★

Ever since 1763, when seven years of French and Indian War ended, England and her North American colonists had been testing each other. Did Parliament have the right to tax the Americans?

On a bitter December night in 1773 the Sons of Liberty dumped English tea into Boston Harbor rather than pay the hated tea tax.

"Tea stands for tyranny!" they shouted.

"It stands for treason," King George replied. He closed the port city and sent his red-coated soldiers and men-of-war to keep the peace. By the following September, colonial delegates, including John Adams of Massachusetts, had gathered in Philadelphia to discuss the crisis at the First Continental Congress. When they came together again in May 1775, shots had been fired at Lexington, and the Second Continental Congress quickly became the governing body of a little country going to war against the most powerful empire in the world.

CONCORD

The villagers hid weapons and gunpowder in their attics, cellars and haylofts

LINCOLN

JOHN ADAMS
atty. at law

N ow hold it thisaway, young feller!" Johnny Adams straightened up the heavy musket as the ragged militiaman watched with a keen squint.

"That's the ticket!" Johnny felt a hard thump of approval on his back.

"When I come back this way you'll be doin' the manual of arms good as any soldier."

LEXINGTON

PAUL REVERE rides the BATTLE ROAD

MEDFORD

BRITISH Patrols capture PAUL REVERE — BILLY DAWES escaped

MONATAMY

MALDEN

There was fierce fighting all along the road to Boston.

MYSTIC RIVER

BUNKER HILL

All the long hot day of **JUNE 17, 1775**, the rebels defended the fort they built on Breed's Hill the night before. The English won a terrible victory as Johnny Adams and his mother watched from the top of PENN's HILL. This battle became known as the **BATTLE of BUNKER HILL**.

The King's Gen. Goge had to keep the peace in angry Bay Colony. He sent 700 soldiers to CONCORD to seize the rebels' military supplies. The SONS of LIBERTY signalled Paul Revere with lanterns in the Old North Church steeple. Billy Dawes was already on his way. Fighting between the BRITISH and the Americans began at **Lexington and Concord APRIL 18·19 1775**

CHARLESTOWN

CAMBRIDGE

BREED'S HILL

OLD NORTH CHURCH

CHARLES RIVER

BOSTON

BOSTON HARBOR

BOSTON NECK

Dorchester Heights

BILLY DAWES rides from the South.

BROOKLINE

ROXBURY

THE Rebel militia had a camp here.

NANTASKET ROADS

1 2 3 4
a scale of miles

N

QUINCY BAY

HINGHAM BAY

DEDHAM

WOLLASTON

HOUGH'S NECK

JOHN ADAMS WAS BORN IN THIS HOUSE —

BRAINTREE

HINGHAM

MILTON

BLUE HILLS

JOHN and ABIGAIL ADAMS and their children lived in this house next door. Their home was called PENN's HILL FARM!

'PENN'S HILL

STOUGHTON

WEYMOUTH

MILTON HILLS

PHILADELPHIA

PLYMOUTH

With that, he shouldered his pack and said, "I'll thank your ma for breakfast and lettin' me bed down in your barn. Send my regards to your pa at the Congress in Philadelphia."

"Yes, sir," said Johnny proudly.

"I know he'll do right by us." The soldier stuck out his whiskery chin. "Ol' King George thought we was a passel of hayseeds who couldn't fight! He found out different at Lexington and Breed's Hill."

Then the soldier stretched his lean legs up the dusty road that led to the army camp at Roxbury. Johnny watched him out of sight and went into the house.

There was a family of strangers in the parlor, folding up their quilts. Everyone in the villages around Boston was making room for folks like these. Patriots, they were running away from the British troops that controlled Boston. But some people were going *to* the city for protection in case of war. They were Tories, determined to stick by the King.

"Ma?" Johnny called.

"Up here."

Johnny followed her voice up the twisting stairway.

Ma was at her little writing desk by the window in her and Pa's bedroom.

Johnny liked the sound of Ma's goose quill scratching black ink across white paper. He studied Ma's face. It was pale and pointy like his. Grown-ups told him all the time, "John Quincy, you have your mother's brown eyes."

"Are you writing to Pa?"

"Yes," she answered as the quill pen continued its scratching.

The postrider would sound his horn as he approached a village. Here comes the mail!

"Your father's homesick and worried about us, what with all the war rumors, and a week at best for the rider to carry a letter from us to him."

"When's he coming home?"

"May be months," she sighed, and dipped her quill into the inkstand.

"Are you going to ask him to send you some pins? I heard you tell Nabby that ever since the soldiers closed the port, you couldn't get sewing pins for love nor money. Maybe Pa could buy you some in Philadelphia?"

Ma smiled. "Perhaps, though he probably has enough on his mind, arguing with all the other gentlemen at the Congress and trying to organize an army."

"Did you tell him Charley wants to be a soldier?"

Ma looked at him sideways. She set her goose quill in its stand and gave him a squeeze. "Yes, John Quincy. Now run along." She laughed. "I'll tell Pa you send your regards."

"That soldier sends his, too."

Out behind the house, Patty, the freckle-faced hired girl, was hanging the wash. Johnny's little brothers, Charley and Tommy, were running between the wet, flapping sheets. As Johnny pumped a bucket of water, he thought how much fun it would be to run and play with them. But now that he was eight years old, and Pa was away, there was lots of work to do on the farm.

His big sister, Nabby, was named after their mother, Abigail, but she looked like their stocky father. Being the oldest, she was bossy sometimes, but Johnny mostly liked her. She sat back on her heels between the rows of potato plants and wiped her smudged face on her sleeve. "Ma said to be sure you water the peas."

"I wish the redcoats would attack, and we'd have to fly to the woods like Pa wrote in his letter," Johnny replied darkly.

"John Quincy, you say horrible things!"

They were both laughing when Ma came out to the garden, tying the ribbons of her straw bonnet.

"Patty and I are off to market. There are bound to be hungry travelers this evening, poor souls."

"What about the people in the parlor?" asked Johnny.

"They just left. They have relatives down in Plymouth. The ladies will be here for quilting today, Nabby." As Ma and Patty headed for the stable, Ma said, "Charley, you and Tommy be good and keep the chickens out of the garden!"

"We will, Mama." Chasing squawking chickens was what they liked best of all. When the farm wagon creaked away, Nabby said, "She is lonely for Pa."

Johnny went to fetch more water. He felt as if they were all on an island.

When Pa came home a month later, he brought the outside world. The family hugged one another close in the circle of his arms.

"How long can you stay, Pa?" asked Nabby.

"Only until September, Miss Bright Eyes."

Ma kissed Pa's cheek. "It's three weeks better than nothing. Let's take a picnic up on Penn's Hill. We'll watch the sunset, and you can tell us the news."

George Washington had led VIRGINIA'S Colonial troops against the FRENCH in the wilderness of OHIO and PENNSYLVANIA. Since 1759, he had been a farmer and legislator in the House of Burgesses. There he got to know the brilliant Thomas Jefferson.

John Dickinson of PENNSYLVANIA was convinced that all could be worked out between the Colonies and the Crown.

Freethinking Benjamin Franklin of Philadelphia represented American interests in England for 15 years then came home to join the Revolution.

The red sunset glinted off their pewter plates. Pa puffed his pipe and told them about the famous Mr. Franklin, a Pennsylvania delegate, and tall, redheaded Tom Jefferson of Virginia. They argued long and hard with conservative delegates, who were dead set against independence. "We sent the King a peace proposal, but he refused it!" Pa's lips were pressed together, thin and defiant. "When our colonial troops fought together against the British on Breed's Hill, we were born as a nation! But, my dears," he continued in a softer voice, "the people are not ready for the fight ahead of us."

"You were right to nominate General Washington to lead
the army," Ma soothed. She leaned her head on Pa's shoulder.
The evening breeze ruffled her linen cap.

They listened to the crickets and watched lamplights ap-
pear in the village below. Soon they made their way home-
ward down the hill. Charley and Tommy slept in Ma's and
Pa's arms. Nabby and Johnny carried the picnic basket.

Too soon the morning came when Pa had to return to Philadelphia. Johnny, squeezed in a bear hug, breathed in Pa's scent of books and pipe tobacco. He tried to remember it as summer turned to fall and fall turned to winter. In Boston and in the villages nearby, there were hard times and sickness. Lots of people died, even Patty. Icy winds blew in from the ocean.

Johnny and Nabby studied their lessons at Pa's law table close by the fire as a winter storm roared in the chimney. Charley was practicing his writing on the frosty window when he shouted, "Someone's coming! He's riding a big black horse!"

Pa burst into the room. His cape and his hat were covered with snow. "Merry Christmas!" he boomed. His saddlebags were full of presents: books from Philadelphia and handkerchiefs from Spain. Pa's cheeks were red with cold.

"How did you get away?" Ma asked. "The Congress is still in session?"

Pa stretched his stockinged feet close to the fire. "Yes, but I asked leave to go." He filled his pipe. "I missed my family, and I had to bring you these, my dear," he said, taking a small bundle from his waistcoat.

"Pins!" Johnny cried.

When Pa returned to the Congress, he sent Ma a copy of
an angry pamphlet written by Mr. Paine that she read to her
friends as they sewed in the afternoons. They'd long since
folded away their quilt frames. Now they were weaving and
sewing woolen coats for the army. Nabby knitted stockings
as Ma read, " '. . . A government of our own is a natural
right.' " Ma added tartly, "I hope that government will in-
clude laws to protect us."

"Yes," said the women.

Johnny listened to hot, angry talk in the cold meetinghouse. The King had ordered his navy to capture American ships. He hired thirty thousand German soldiers called Hessians to put down the rebellious colonists. "We'll have independence!" the men shouted. Johnny heard other talk: There were Tory rumors that Pa had turned traitor and sailed for England.

As Johnny thumped down a load of firewood, Ma scrubbed the kitchen floor furiously, as if the Tory gossipers and King George himself were beneath her scrub brush.

All the moon-bright night of March 4, 1776, booms like thunder from the north rattled the windows of the Adamses' house. Charley and Tommy curled up tight with Johnny under the blankets.

"What's going to happen, Johnny?" they whispered.

"I don't know. Try to go to sleep."

"Are soldiers going to come? Are they?"

"I don't know," Johnny whispered. He wished he did.

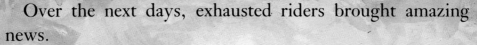

Over the next days, exhausted riders brought amazing news.

"General Washington surrounded the town! With cannons hauled clear from Fort Ticonderoga," one rider panted. "His Lordship is taking his troops and his Tories and they're pullin' out of Boston!"

"Hurrah!" the people shouted.

On the morning of the seventeenth, the Adams children stood with Ma and their neighbors on top of Penn's Hill to watch the hated British ships sail from misty Boston Harbor.

"It's like a forest of masts," Ma said. "Now Boston is ours again. We'll go there and see what the soldiers have made of our city house and Pa's office."

Because Boston was full of smallpox—more dangerous than soldiers—it was nearly three months before Ma decided they could go to the city.

"We'll stay at Uncle Isaac's house. Aunt Betsy, Aunt Mary, and all the cousins will be there, too. Dr. Bullfinch will give us our smallpox inoculations and we'll all be in quarantine together." Ma looked around the table at them. "Won't that be exciting?"

Johnny and Nabby turned to each other. It would be, they had to agree.

Ma sent a hired hand on ahead with firewood and hay and the cow they would need, and then she drove the wagon loaded with food, bedding, and Adamses the ten bumpy miles to Boston. The last mile was the Neck, a muddy strip of land between the mainland and the city. The road was crowded with travelers.

Ma drove the wagon under the brick archway of the town gate into Boston.

Johnny's eyes and ears were full of fish peddlers, chimney sweeps, and horse hooves on brick and cobblestones. There were church bells, cowbells, and dinner bells. They drove past the Old State House where the Royal Governor had ruled the colony. At last they came to their house on Queen Street.

Chickens had been living in Pa's law office. "Well!" Ma put her hands on her hips. "I'd gladly hand His Majesty a broom and see him clean up the mess his soldiers left behind!"

The following afternoon Ma received a thick envelope from Philadelphia. As Ma began to read, her cheeks flamed. "Everybody, come quick!"

She read in a shaking voice, " 'A Declaration by the Representatives of the United States of America . . .' "

"Independence!" Nabby whispered.

"The King will not let us go lightly," Ma said soberly. "Ready or no, we're at war."

Johnny's heart pounded. The colonies had decided to break away at last, to make war or peace as an independent country. Ma read to them:

" '. . . for the support of this Declaration, with a firm reliance on the protection of Providence, we mutually pledge to each other our lives, our fortunes, and our sacred honor.' "

On the eighteenth day of July, when these words were read to the people of Boston, bells rang all day long. They were answered by thundering salutes fired by the American gunships in the harbor. The Adamses leaned out of their windows to join the cheering.

Down below whiskered soldiers and stout merchants were throwing their hats in the air. The crooked streets of Boston were filled with shouting: "We're our own country now, by jinks! Free and independent!"

Johnny smiled up at his mother. Her brown eyes were shining, just like his.

The American Revolution

What had Pa been doing all this time?

When the colonial delegates first got together at the Continental Congress in September 1774, they were mostly interested in fair treatment from Great Britain. They thought of themselves as Englishmen. By the spring of 1776, the stubborn Parliament in London was forcing them to face serious questions—as Americans.

How should the thirteen colonies govern themselves? How should they trade and get along with one another, with England, with other countries? And the dangerous question of independence was being talked about more and more. It would mean war and poverty, "like destroying our house in winter before we have got another shelter," said Mr. Dickinson of Pennsylvania.

On the seventh of June, 1776, Richard Henry Lee of Virginia resolved that the "United Colonies" ought to be free and independent states. If the Congress agreed, there would have to be an official declaration to tell the world why this bold breaking away was just common sense.

John Adams, Benjamin Franklin, Thomas Jefferson, Roger Sherman, and Robert Livingston were chosen to work it out. Pa told Mr. Jefferson he had better put their thoughts into words: "You can write ten times better than I can." So he did. But by the time it was finished, nearly everyone had had a say.

The Declaration of Independence was approved by the Congress on July 4, 1776. This is how it begins:

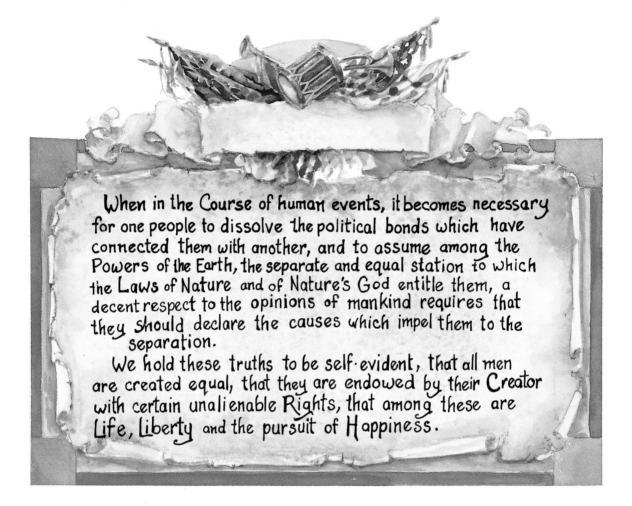

When in the Course of human events, it becomes necessary for one people to dissolve the political bonds which have connected them with another, and to assume among the Powers of the Earth, the separate and equal station to which the Laws of Nature and of Nature's God entitle them, a decent respect to the opinions of mankind requires that they should declare the causes which impel them to the separation.

We hold these truths to be self-evident, that all men are created equal, that they are endowed by their Creator with certain unalienable Rights, that among these are Life, Liberty and the pursuit of Happiness.

The glorious Independence Days were followed by six hard years of a war that was nearly lost more than once. Nine-year-old Johnny Adams became a post rider on the Braintree-to-Boston road. Two years later when the Congress sent Pa to Paris to represent America, Johnny went along as Pa's secretary. The United States was too broke to hire one.

All through the American towns and backcountry forests there was bitter fighting between soldiers, settlers, and Indians. Seeing the British as the lesser of twin evils, the native tribes generally sided with them. The most feared tribes were the Iroquois, led by Thayendanehea, war chief of the Mohawks. His English name was Joseph Brant. He traveled to England and met King George. They became friends.

After the taking of BOSTON, Gen. Washington suffered many defeats in NEW YORK and NEW JERSEY. All through the war, he never had enough soldiers nor food and uniforms for those he had. They retreated into PENNSYLVANIA.

Late Christmas night 1776, the General and his freezing hungry troops crossed back over the icy Delaware River to Trenton, NEW JERSEY. The Patriots beat the GERMAN soldiers hired by ENGLAND. The REVOLUTION was saved at its darkest hour.

Gen. George Washington

The AMERICANS were never able to capture QUEBEC JAN 1, 1776

Nathan Hale was captured as a spy in New York and executed SEP 22, 1775. "I only regret that I have but one life to lose for my country"

FORT TICONDEROGA

The TURNING POINT After British General "Gentleman Johnny" BURGOYNE surrendered at SARATOGA, the FRENCH decided to join the rebellious PATRIOTS.

SARATOGA OCT 17, 1777

BENNINGTON AUG 16, 1777

BOSTON MAR 17, 1776

Sept 1780. When Gen. Benedict Arnold went over to the BRITISH, the AMERICANS nearly lost their fort at WEST POINT.

The Marquis de Lafayette volunteered his services to General Washington and the armies of the new nation.

The Continental Army spent a terrible winter at VALLEY FORGE

LONG ISLAND AUG 27, 1776

NEW YORK CITY SEP 15, 1776

MONMOUTH JUN 28 1778

GERMANTOWN OCT 4, 1777

TRENTON DEC 26, 1776

BRANDYWINE SEP 11, 1777

PHILADELPHIA SEP 26, 1777

the COMTE de ROCHAMBEAU COMMANDER of FRENCH forces IN AMERICA

At Monmouth Courthouse, Molly Pitcher took her wounded husband's place at his gun and became a legend.

From the summer of 1778 until the winter of 1779, George Rogers Clark led a band of KENTUCKY "Long Knives" in a victorious campaign through the OLD NORTHWEST TERRITORY

The BRITISH commander, Gen. Clinton was expecting an attack at New York but Gen. Washington fooled him. 17,000 FRENCH and AMERICAN troops trapped Gen. Cornwallis at Yorktown, VIRGINIA. The BRITISH Surrendered OCT 19, 1781.

YORKTOWN

VINCENNES FEB 23-25 1779

KASKASKIA JUL 4, 1778

GUILFORD COURTHOUSE MAR 15, 1781

After CAMDEN, young General Nathanael Greene of RHODE ISLAND took over command of the hungry AMERICANS—too weak to win, too stubborn to give up.

KINGS MOUNTAIN OCT 7, 1780

COWPENS JAN 17, 1781

CAMDEN AUG 16, 1780

Lord Charles CORNWALLIS

24 FRENCH ships stop 19 ships of the ENGLISH FLEET at Chesapeake Bay Sep 5, 1781

Gen. Horatio Gates and 3000 worn-out Continentals were defeated at CAMDEN, SOUTH CAROLINA by Gen. Charles, Lord Cornwallis

CHARLES TOWN MAY 11, 1780

COMMANDERS-IN-CHIEF BRITISH FORCES IN AMERICA

Sir William HOWE

Sir Henry CLINTON

Gen. Howe was replaced by the cautious Gen. Clinton in 1778.

SAVANNAH OCT 9, 1779

● AMERICAN victories
● BRITISH victories

● a draw

Most of the blacks who lived in the colonies were owned by white Americans, so they may well have been on the British side, too. But nearly five thousand blacks, slave and free, fought with the Continental army and distinguished themselves in battle.

John Quincy studied hard in Europe. By the time he was fourteen, in 1781, he became secretary to the first U.S. ambassador to the Russian court at St. Petersburg.

Back home, delegates from the not very United States were forming a government. Their agreement, the Articles of Confederation, let each state run its own business.

John Quincy returned to Massachusetts in 1784 to complete his studies at Harvard College. His father was unable to return to America until 1788; he missed seeing John Quincy's graduation in 1787 and was unable to take part when fifty-five delegates gathered once more in Philadelphia to write a new law of the land.

Alexander Hamilton, George Washington, and James Madison became dissatisfied with the Articles and thought a stronger central government ought to be organized.

When ten amendments were agreed upon in 1791, all of the states agreed to be governed by the Constitution. These amendments are called the Bill of Rights. They protect the citizens from a too-powerful government and guarantee such personal liberties as freedom of speech. The people's wishes for a free, self-governing nation were fulfilled at last. The Constitution begins like this:

We the People of the United States, in order to form a more perfect Union, establish justice, insure domestic tranquility, provide for the common defense, promote the general welfare, and secure the blessings of liberty to ourselves and our posterity, do ordain and establish this Constitution for the United States of America.

1787

George Washington was chosen to lead the country in 1789. After John Adams served two terms as his vice president, Adams himself was narrowly elected to the highest office. A peaceful passing of power from one elected leader to another: That was truly revolutionary.

John and Abigail Adams were the first to live in the half-finished White House.
Abigail hung her wet laundry to dry in the East Room.

As a diplomat in Europe, John Quincy Adams earned respect for himself and his country. In 1817, he became Secretary of State for President James Monroe.

By the stormy presidential campaign of 1824, Abigail, Charley, and Nabby had died. John Adams was ninety years old when he and his youngest son, Thomas, saw John Quincy become the sixth president of the United States.

Over the years John Quincy had become a grim, stubborn man who liked to skinny-dip in the Potomac River. Both he and his father made lots of enemies, including Thomas Jefferson and Andrew Jackson, who became presidents when the Adamses weren't re-elected. But John Adams made peace with his old friend. In 1826, he and Thomas Jefferson passed away on the same summer day, the Fourth of July.

After his one-term presidency, and for the rest of his life, John Quincy Adams served in the House of Representatives. The child of the Revolution died there "at his post of duty," February 23, 1848. He was eighty years old.

BIBLIOGRAPHY

Bowen, Catherine Drinker. *John Adams and the American Revolution*. Boston: Little, Brown & Co., 1950.

Butterfield, L. H., M. Friedlander, and M. J. Kline, eds. *The Book of Abigail and John (Selected Letters)*. Cambridge, Mass.: Harvard University Press, 1975.

*Carter, Alden R. *Darkest Hours*. New York: Franklin Watts, 1988.

*Copeland, Peter F. *Everyday Dress of the American Colonial Period*. New York: Dover Publications, 1975. Coloring book.

*Epstein, Sam, and Beryl Epstein. *Young Paul Revere's Boston*. Champaign, Ill.: Garrard Publishing Co., 1966.

Forbes, Esther. *Paul Revere and the World He Lived in*. Boston: Houghton Mifflin Co., 1942.

Ketchum, Richard M., ed. *The American Heritage Book of the Revolution*. New York: American Heritage Publishing Co., 1958.

McDowell, Bart. *The Revolutionary War*. Washington: National Geographic Society, 1967.

*Ross, George E. *Know Your Declaration of Independence and the 56 Signers*. Chicago: Rand McNally & Co., 1963.

Stone, Irving. *Those Who Love*. Garden City, N.Y.: Doubleday & Co., 1965.

*Books especially written for young readers

"Old Man Eloquent" was his nickname.